Australian Police Vehicles

Aaron White

www.facebook.com/childrensbooksbyaaronwhite
www.childrensbooksbyaaronwhite.com

DEDICATION

I dedicate this book to my beautiful wife, Francesca, and to my wonderful sons, Tyler and Jayden. I also dedicate it to all of the Fantastic Police Officers. You men and women do such an amazing job, and I hope this book will help to show people what you do. Thank you.

Copyright © 2017 Aaron White
All rights reserved.

ISBN-13: 978-0-9943915-3-7

The Australian Police Force uses lots of different vehicles and animals to keep Australia safe. Come and meet some of these Awesome Vehicles and Animals.

We will start with Peter, the Patrol Car.

Hi, I'm Peter, the Patrol Car. I drive around the streets making sure that all of the other vehicles are doing the right thing. If they are driving too fast, I turn on my red and blue flashing lights to tell them to slow down.

My name is Belinda, the Boat. I sail along the water and make sure that all of the other boats and jet skis are doing the right thing. If they are in an area that is unsafe, I let them know and ask them to, please, move along.

I like helping the other boats.

Hello, I'm Michelle, the Motorcycle. I ride past the cars and see if the driver is on their mobile phone. If they are, I put on my red and blue flashing lights, and tell them to stop looking at their phone, or they might cause a crash.

Hi, I am Harry, the Helicopter. If a vehicle is running away from the police, I can fly up into the sky to get a better view. Then, I can let my friends, Peter and Michelle, know where the vehicle is going so they can stop it.

G'day, I'm Vince, the Dog Van. I carry my friend, Dean, the Dog around in a safe carrier in the back of me.

Dean is so cool. He can sniff out explosives, which can be very dangerous in the wrong hands.

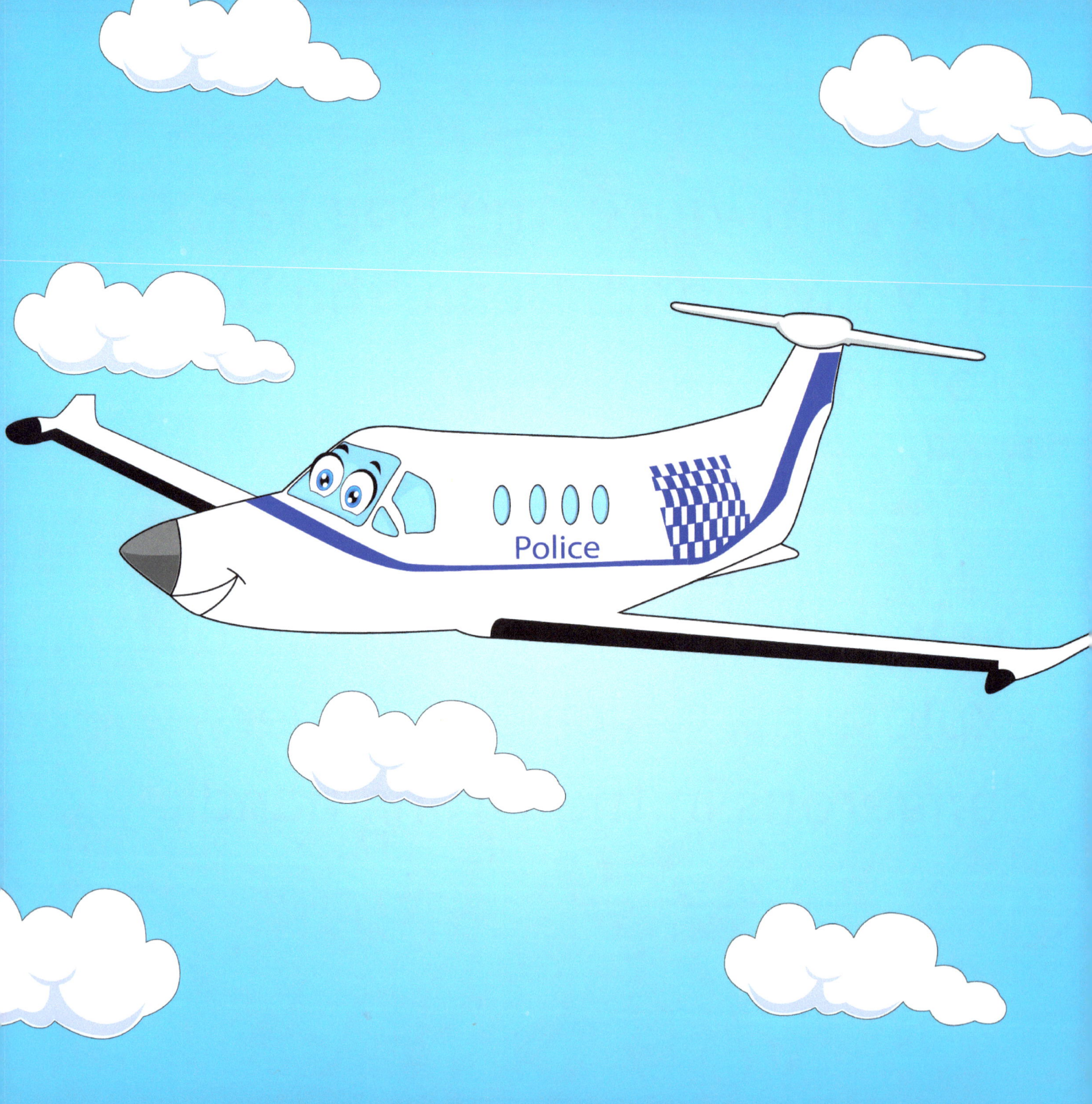

I am Andrew, the Airplane. If a person is lost, I can fly up into the sky to get a better view of the area and, hopefully, find them.

Also, if another plane is doing something it shouldn't be doing, I can fly up to them and tell them to stop.

G'day, I'm Richard, the Armoured Rescue Vehicle. If someone needs rescuing from a dangerous situation, like a bank robbery, I can help.

I am bullet and blast resistant. That is pretty awesome.

Hello, I am Bronwyn, the Booze Bus. I block off the road and test the drivers of the vehicles to make sure they have not drunk too much alcohol. This is because if they have, they may cause a crash.

Neigh, I'm Helen, the Horse. I walk around the parks and festivals to make sure everyone is behaving themselves. If they are not, I say "Neigh, stop acting silly."

I am Wayne, the Paddy Wagon. I transport people who have broken the law to the police station.

Laws have been made to keep everyone safe and to let everyone know how they should treat each other. That is, with respect.

Here is the Police Station. It is a building where some of the police vehicles live.

If you ever need help due to someone breaking the law, you can come inside and ask a friendly police officer for help.

They love helping people.

I hope that was fun, meeting and learning about all of those Fantastic Police Vehicles and Animals.

I have left some blank pages for you to draw your favourite police vehicles and animals on.